Fetch more tail wagging recipes
and pup-approved treats, visit

www.FetchandRead.com

Introduction

Our furry friends bring so much joy into our lives and deserve the best we can give them!

That's why I created this collection of tasty and nutritious homemade treats that you can easily make for your beloved pup.

Each recipe is crafted with simple, wholesome ingredients that not only taste great, but also provide real health benefits.

I hope you and your dog enjoy these homemade goodies as much as I enjoyed creating them!

Why Cook for Your Dog?

Healthier Ingredients:
You control what goes into every bite—no hidden fillers or harmful additives.

Tailored to Your Pup:
Recipes can be adjusted for your dog's size, preferences, or dietary needs.

Bonding Time
Cooking for your dog is an act of love, and they'll feel it every time you share one of these homemade goodies.

Cost-Effective
Many recipes use affordable, everyday ingredients—saving money compared to premium store-bought treats.

Peace of Mind
You'll know exactly what your pup is eating, ensuring their snacks are both safe and delicious.

INGREDIENTS & BENEFITS

Ground Turkey & Chicken	Lean protein, supports muscle health, low in fat.
Zucchini	Low-calorie veggie, high in vitamins A & C, aids digestion.
Oats	Good source of fiber, supports digestion and steady energy release.
Eggs	Provides protein and healthy fats, supports skin and coat health.
Wheat/Oat Flour	Gluten-free, gentle on digestion, provides energy.
Banana	Rich in potassium, magnesium, and natural sweetness for energy.
Unsalted Peanut Butter	Healthy fats and protein, encourages shiny coats.

INGREDIENTS & BENEFITS

Carrots	Great for teeth-cleaning crunch, rich in vitamin A for vision and immune health.
Parsley	Freshens breath, natural source of vitamins K and C.
Broccoli	High in vitamin C, calcium, and fiber; supports bone and immune health.
Sweet Potatoes	Rich in dietary fiber, beta-carotene, and antioxidants; great for digestion and immune system.
Coconut Oil	Contains medium-chain fatty acids for skin, coat, and brain health.
Pumpkin Puree	High in fiber, great for digestion, helps with firm stools.

INGREDIENTS & BENEFITS

Ingredient	Benefit
Shredded Cheddar Cheese	Calcium and protein, though bes in moderation.
Low-fat Mozzarella Sticks	Calcium and protein; low-fat option is easier on digestion.
Chicken Breast	Lean protein for muscle support.
Olive Oil	Healthy fat, supports coat shine and heart health.
Applesauce	Natural sweetness, vitamins A & C, low in fat.
Flaxseed	Omega-3s, fiber, supports healthy skin and coat.
Greek Yogurt	Probiotics for gut health, protein, and calcium.

INGREDIENTS & BENEFITS

Blueberries	Antioxidants, fiber, vitamin C, brain-boosting.
Strawberries	High in vitamin C, fiber, supports immune system.
Apple	Vitamin A & C, fiber, natual sweetness (safe without seeds)
Salmon	Omega-3 fatty acids, supports skin, coat, and joints.
Tuna	Protein and omega-3s, supports muscles and coat.

Disclaimer

Please research all recipes and ingredients to ensure they are safe for your dog. Consult your veterinarian to address any concerns or special dietary needs.

Prior to cooking, it's advised to check your dog for food allergies. Monitor them when introducing any new treats.

Foods to Avoid

- Chocolate
- Grapes & raisins
- Avocado
- Garlic & onions
- Macadamia nuts
- Xylitol

RECIPES

🍗 Protein Bites
Pup-peroni Poppers
Woofles
Chicken Nibble Nuggets

🥕 Veggie Snacks
Carrot Crunchies
Broccoli Bark Bites
Sweet Paw-tato Chips

🧀 Cheesy Treats
Cheddar Chompers
Mozza-Mutt Sticks

🍌 Fruity Munchies
Banana Pupcakes
Berry Good Bites
Apple Snaps

🐟 Seafood-Inspired
Salmon Sniffers
Tuna Twisties

🎉 Fun Party Treats
Tail-Wag Tacos
Bow-Wow Bruschetta

Pup-peroni Poppers

INGREDIENTS

1/2 lb ground turkey or chicken

1/2 cup shredded zucchini

1/4 cup rolled oats

1 egg

INSTRUCTIONS

- Preheat oven to 375°F.
- Squeeze out excess moisture from zucchini.
- In a bowl, combine all ingredients.
- Roll mixture into small meatballs.
- Place on lined baking sheet.
- Bake for 20–25 minutes, until cooked through.

Woofles

Ingredients:

- 🐾 1 cup oat flour
- 🐾 1 ripe banana, mashed
- 🐾 1/4 cup peanut butter
- 🐾 1/4 cup water

Instructions

1. Preheat waffle iron.
2. In a bowl, combine oat flour, banana, peanut butter, and water.
3. Mix until well combined.
4. Spoon batter into waffle iron and cook until golden brown.

Chicken Nibble Nuggets

INGREDIENTS

1 pound boneless, skinless chicken breast

½ cup grated carrot

1 large egg

DIRECTIONS

1. Preheat oven to 350°F (175 C).

2. Cut the chicken into small cubes.

3. In a bowl, combine the chicken, carrot, and egg

4. Place mixture on a baking sheet and press into a flat, even layer. Bake for 15–20 minutes. Let cool, then cut into small cubes.

CARROT CRUNCHIES

INGREDIENTS

- 2 large carrots
- 1 tsp chopped parsley

DIRECTIONS

1. Preheat the dehydrator to 135°F (57°C).
2. Slice the carrots into thin rounds.
3. Arrange carrot slices on dehydrator trays.
4. Sprinkle with parsley, then dehydrate for 10-12 hours until crisp.

Broccoli Bark Bites

INGREDIENTS:

2 cups broccoli florets
1 cup rolled oats

INSTRUCTIONS

1. Steam the broccoli florets until tender.
2. Finely chop the broccoli.
3. Place the oats in a shallow bowl.
4. Roll the broccoli florets in the oats until coated.

Sweet Paw-tato Chips

Ingredients

- 2 medium sweet potatoes
- 1 tbsp olive oil

Instructions

1. Preheat oven to 250°F (120°C).
2. Thinly slice the sweet potatoes.
3. Toss with olive oil, then arrange on a lined baking sheet.
4. Bake for 2 ½ to 3 hours, until crisp, flipping halfway.

CHEDDAR CHOMPERS

🐾 Ingredients

- 1 cup oat flour
- ½ cup shredded cheddar cheese
- ¼ cup pumpkin puree

Instructions

1. Preheat oven to 350°F (175°C).
2. In a bowl, combine the oat flour, cheddar, and pumpkin puree.
3. Roll out dough and cut into shapes.
4. Place on a baking sheet and bake for 15-20 minutes.

Mozza-Mutt Sticks

Low-fat mozzarella sticks wrapped in chicken breast and baked.

INGREDIENTS

- 4 low-fat mozzarella sticks
- 8 oz boneless, skinless chicken breast

DIRECTIONS

1. Preheat oven to 350°F (175°C).
2. Cut the chicken into strips.
3. Wrap each mozzarella stick with a strip of chicken
4. Place on a baking sheet and bake for 20-25 minutes.

Banana Pupcakes

Ingredients

1 ripe banana
1 cup oat flour
1/4 cup rolled oats
2 tbsp unsweetened
applesauce

Instructions

- Preheat oven to 350°F.
- In a bowl, mash the banana.
- Add oat flour, oats, and applesauce. Mix well.
- Spoon batter into greased mini muffin tin.
- Bake for 12-15 minutes until golden.

Berry Good Bites

Ingredients

1/2 cup plain yogurt
1/4 cup blueberries
1/4 cup strawberries

Instructions

1. Combine yogurt and berries in a blender
2. Puree until smooth.
3. Drop mixture by small spoonfuls onto a baking sheet.
4. Freeze for 3 hours, or until firm.

Apple Snaps

INGREDIENTS
- 1 apple
- 1/2 cup plain Greek yogurt

INSTRUCTIONS
- Cut apple into slices, removing core and seeds.
- Dip each slice into the yogurt, coating both sides.
- Place slices on a lined baking sheet.
- Freeze for 3 hours or until firm.

Salmon Sniffers

INGREDIENTS

1/2 cup cooked salmon
1/2 cup mashed sweet
potato

INSTRUCTIONS

- In a bowl, combine
  salmon and sweet
  potato.
- Mash together until
  mixed thoroughly.
- Shape mixture into small balls.
- Serve immediately or refrigerate for
  later.

Tuna Twisties

Ingredients

- 1 can tuna, drained
- 1 cup oat flour

Instructions

- Preheat oven to 350°F.

- In a bowl, combine tuna and oat flour. Mix into a dough.

- Roll dough into thin ropes, then form into spirals.

- Bake on lined sheet for 20-25 minutes.

Tail-Wag Tacos

Ingredients:

1/2 cup ground beef

1/4 cup chopped spinach

6 small grain-free tortillas (or lettuce wraps)

Instructions

- In a skillet, cook the beef and spinach.
- Remove from heat and let cool slightly.
- Divide mixture evenly between tortillas.
- Fold over tortillas to serve.

Bow-Wow Bruschetta

Ingredients

- 12 wheat crackers
- 1/3 cup pumpkin puree
- 2 tsp ground flaxseed

Instructions

- Spread pumpkin puree on each cracker, then sprinkle with flaxseed.

Thank You

From the bottom of my heart, thank you for joining me on this journey and for choosing to share these recipes with your pup.

Every recipe in this book was created with love, with the hope that each tail wag, happy bark, and eager lick reminds you of the joy our dogs bring into our lives. They are more than pets, they are family.

By taking the time to make healthy, homemade treats, you're giving your dog more than just food:

You're giving them wellness, by nourishing their bodies with safe, wholesome ingredients.

You're giving them happiness, because good food lifts their mood, brightens their spirit, and fills their day with joy.

Most importantly, you're giving them love. The kind they'll return endlessly, in every cuddle, every wag, and every look that says, "You are my favorite person."

This book isn't just about recipes. it's about deepening the bond between you and your best friend. Healthy treats and meals are one of the many ways to say, "I love you." And dogs, with their big hearts and loyal souls, will love you back a thousand times more for it.

So here's to you, your pup, and the countless moments of happiness these recipes will bring. May every bite remind you of the incredible gift we have in our dogs—unconditional love.